I0541299

If Only Wings Meant Flight

Bahareh Amidi

IF ONLY WINGS MEANT FLIGHT

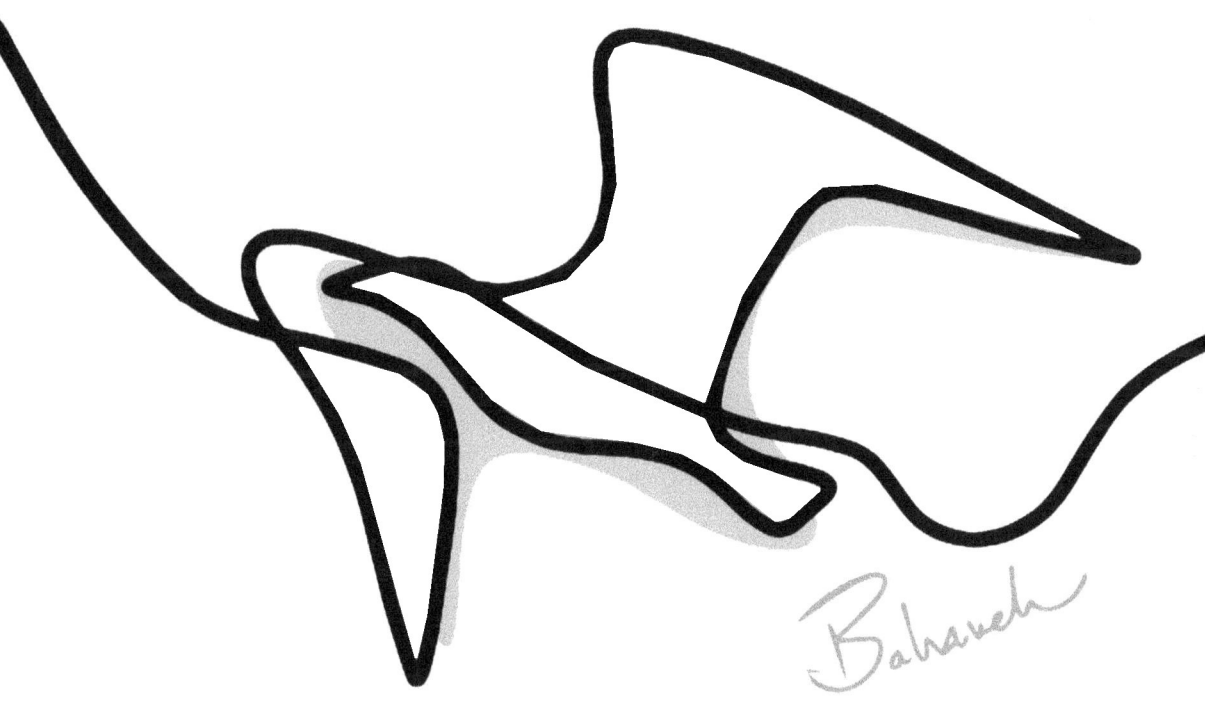

Bahareh

Copyright © 2025 Bahareh Amidi. All Rights Reserved.
ISBN 979-8-9926240-0-7

cover and interior illustrations by
  Adora:
   @AdoraArts

email: connect@bahareh.com
facebook.com/Bahareh.Amidi
twitter.com/BaharehAmidi
youtube.com/baharehLIVE
instagram.com/bahareh_poetess
www.bahareh.com

"Every journey has a secret destination
of which the traveler is unaware"
—Martin Buber

Listen to If Only Wings Meant Flight

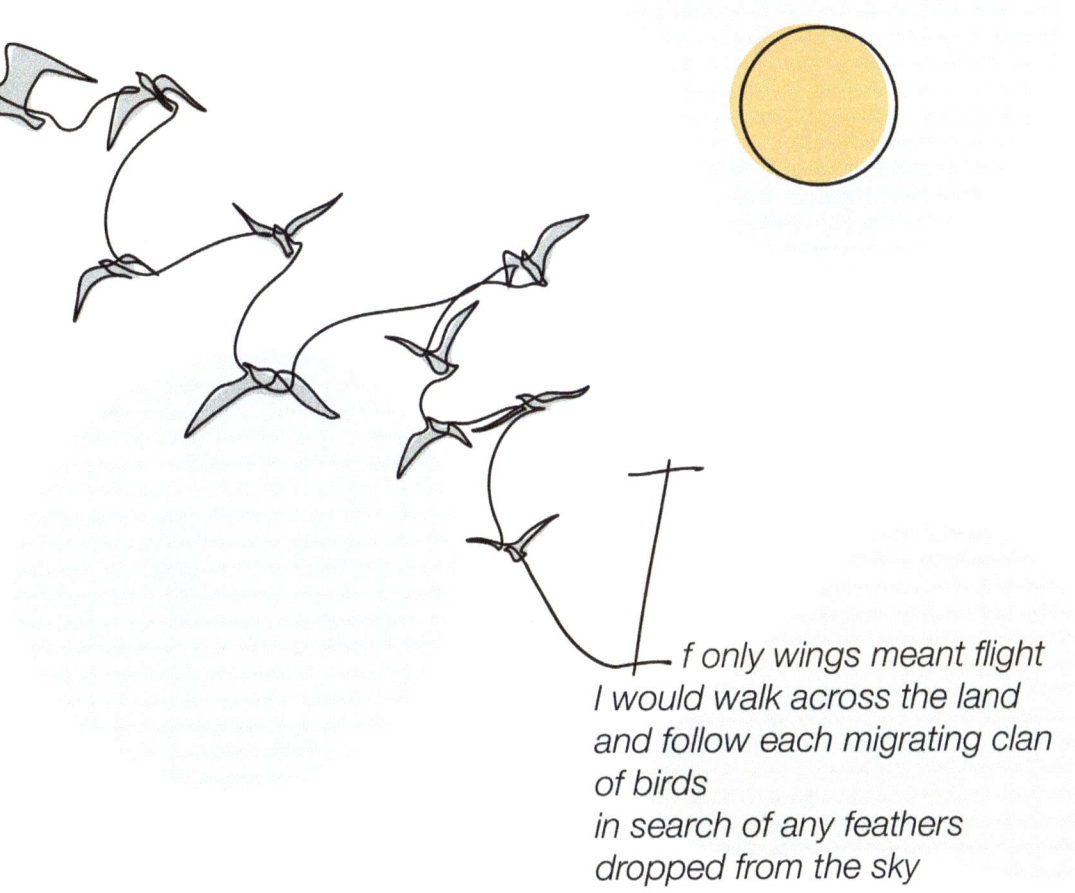

f only wings meant flight
I would walk across the land
and follow each migrating clan
of birds
in search of any feathers
dropped from the sky

If only wings meant flight
I would visit every corner of dark caves
to see if bats have left a dropping
With each sign
I would travel deeper with in
in search of flight.

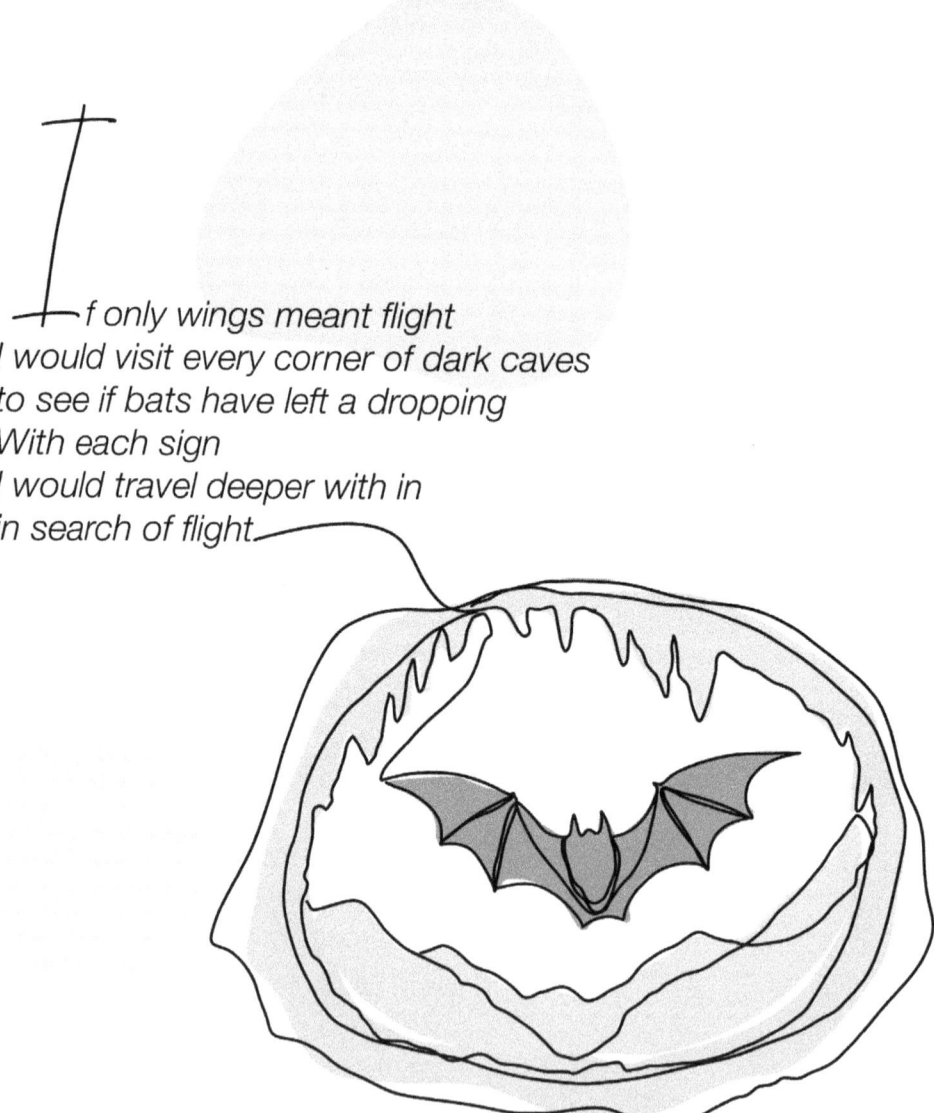

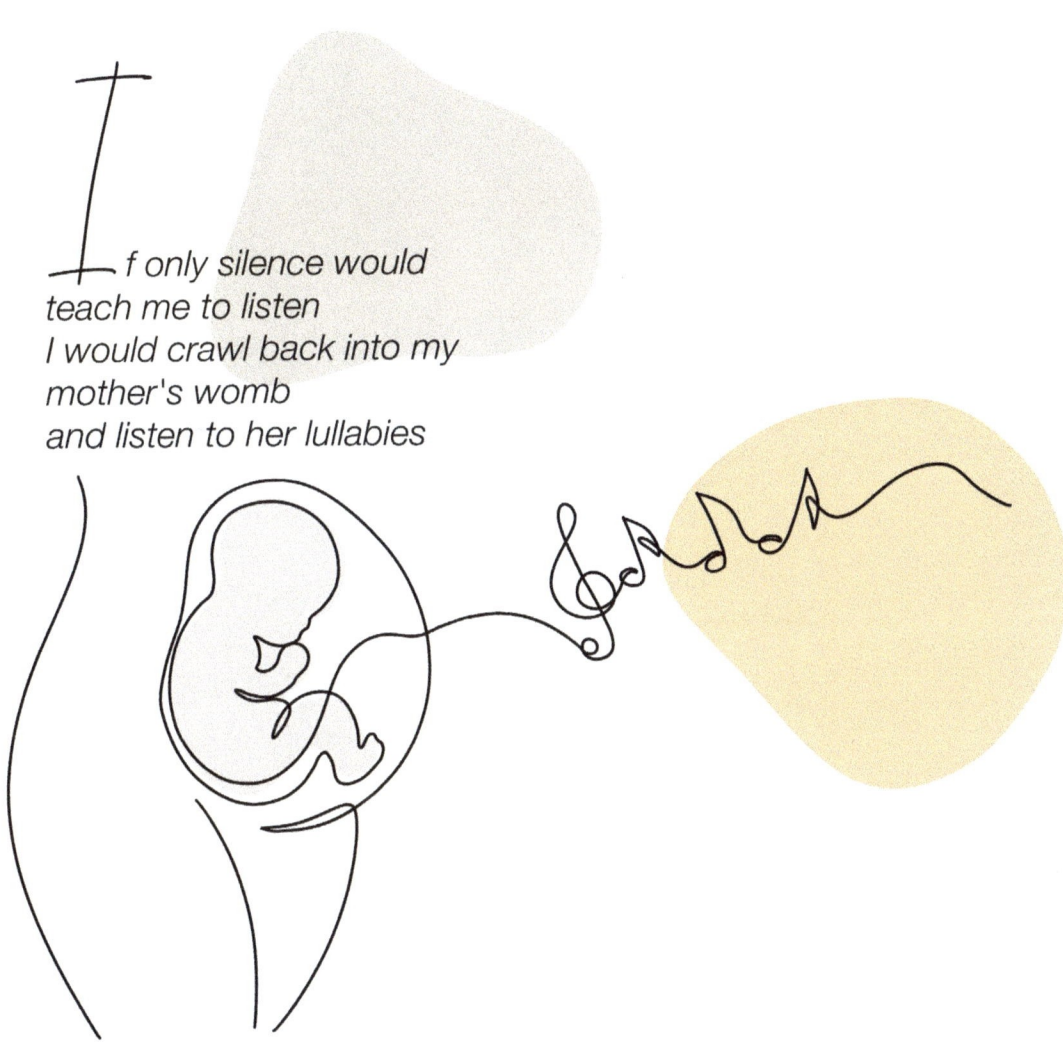

If only silence would
teach me to listen
I would crawl back into my
mother's womb
and listen to her lullabies

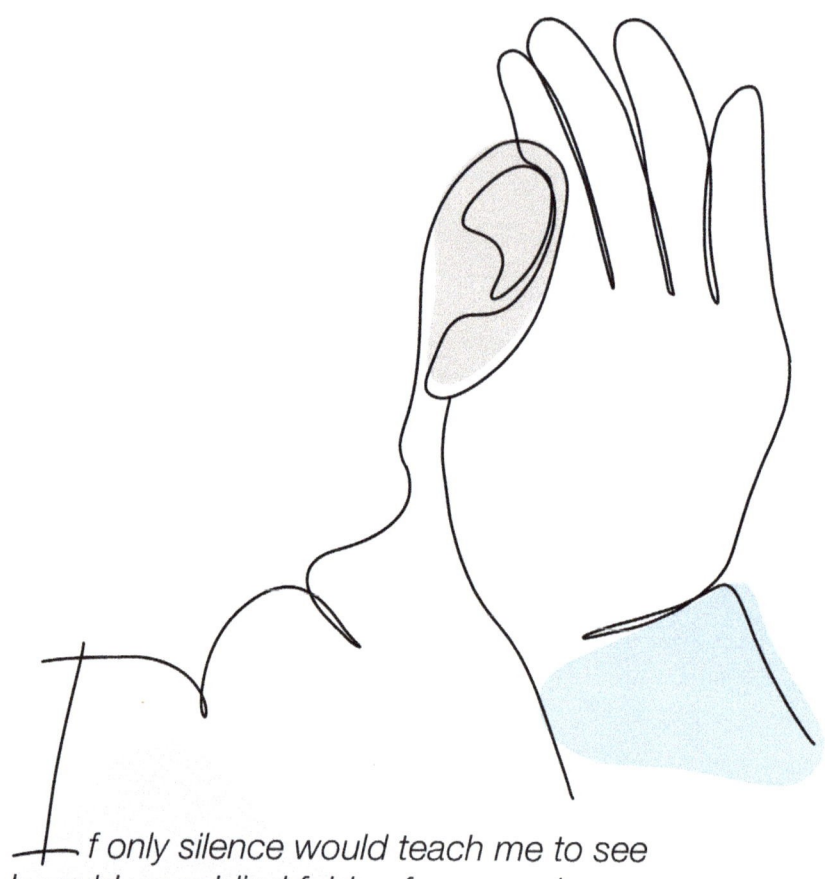

If only silence would teach me to see
I would wear blind folds of many colors
and those colors would tell me the meaning of words
not spoken but heard
Listen

If only wearing white
was the sign of one ready for
pilgrimage
I would paint my skin white
and cover myself with all the
white feathers I had found
and I would wait for the call
to prayer
And for my reception to be
held as I entered the
House of Me

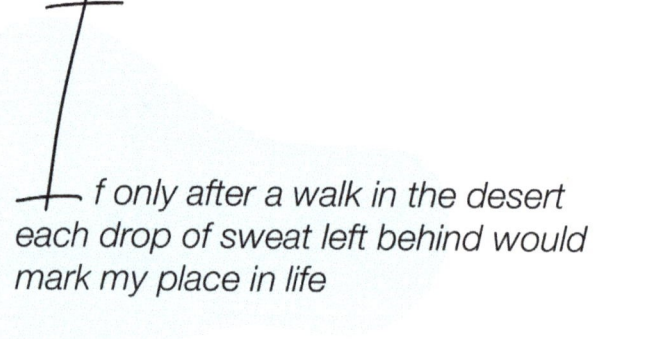

*I f only after a walk in the desert
each drop of sweat left behind would
mark my place in life*

I would go back at night
with a lantern and read
all the maps and the plans
my plain eyes could not see in the day
I can see in the dark

I

f only words meant meaning
I would collect all the dictionaries in the world
and string the words together in prayer
I would wear the strings of words around my neck
in hopes of finding meaning
in what people say but don't mean
Am I deaf or dumb or just not blind

I

f only the word love meant
all the wonderful things hallmark cards
make the word to mean
on Valentine's day

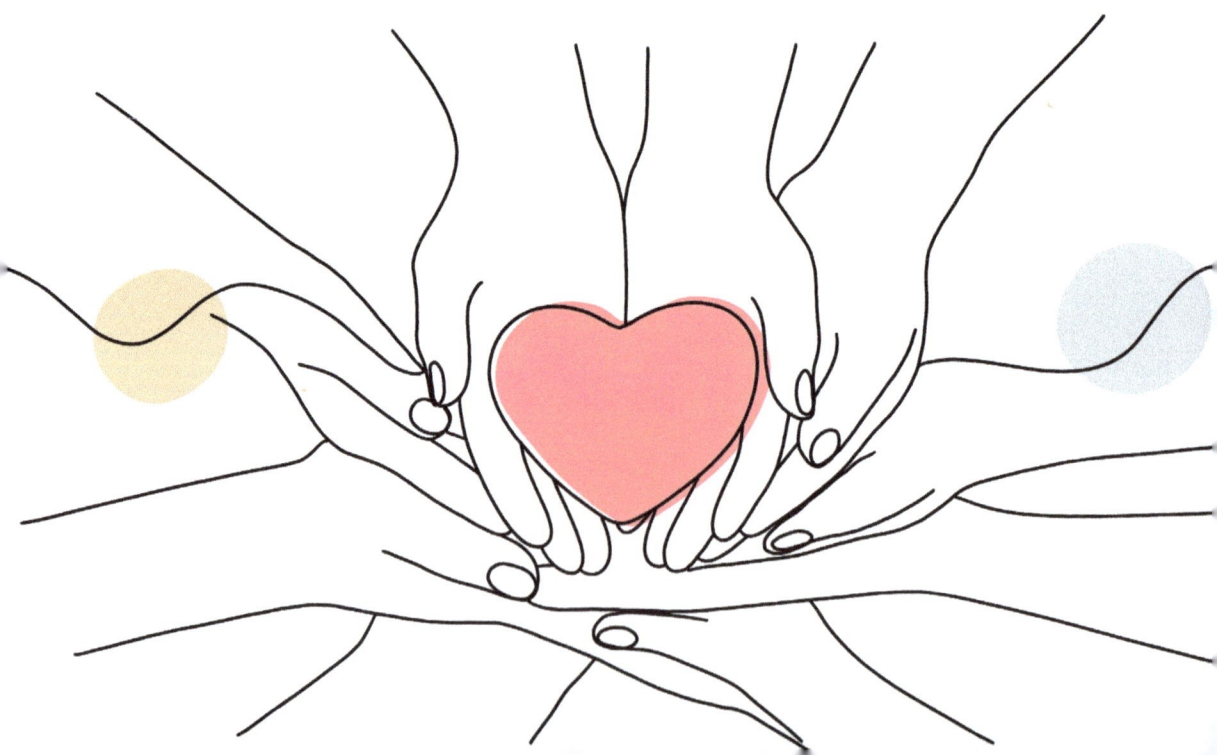

*I*f only Valentine's day
would be dedicated to hate
and all the other days of the year to love
Love would mean Peace

I f only Peace was
not only a sign we would make with our not one
but two fingers raising
And if Peace was not depicted as a rainbow
or a bird carrying grace
Then peace would be felt when eyes actually meet eyes
in greetings that would constitute a prayer

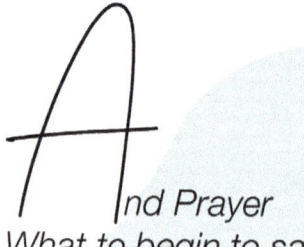

And Prayer
What to begin to say of Prayer
If only we would just abandon all the crosses
and crescents and the stars
If we would leave the houses built
for prayer that are being bombed
Then in our own solitude
in our own temple
we might light a candle and here in Pray

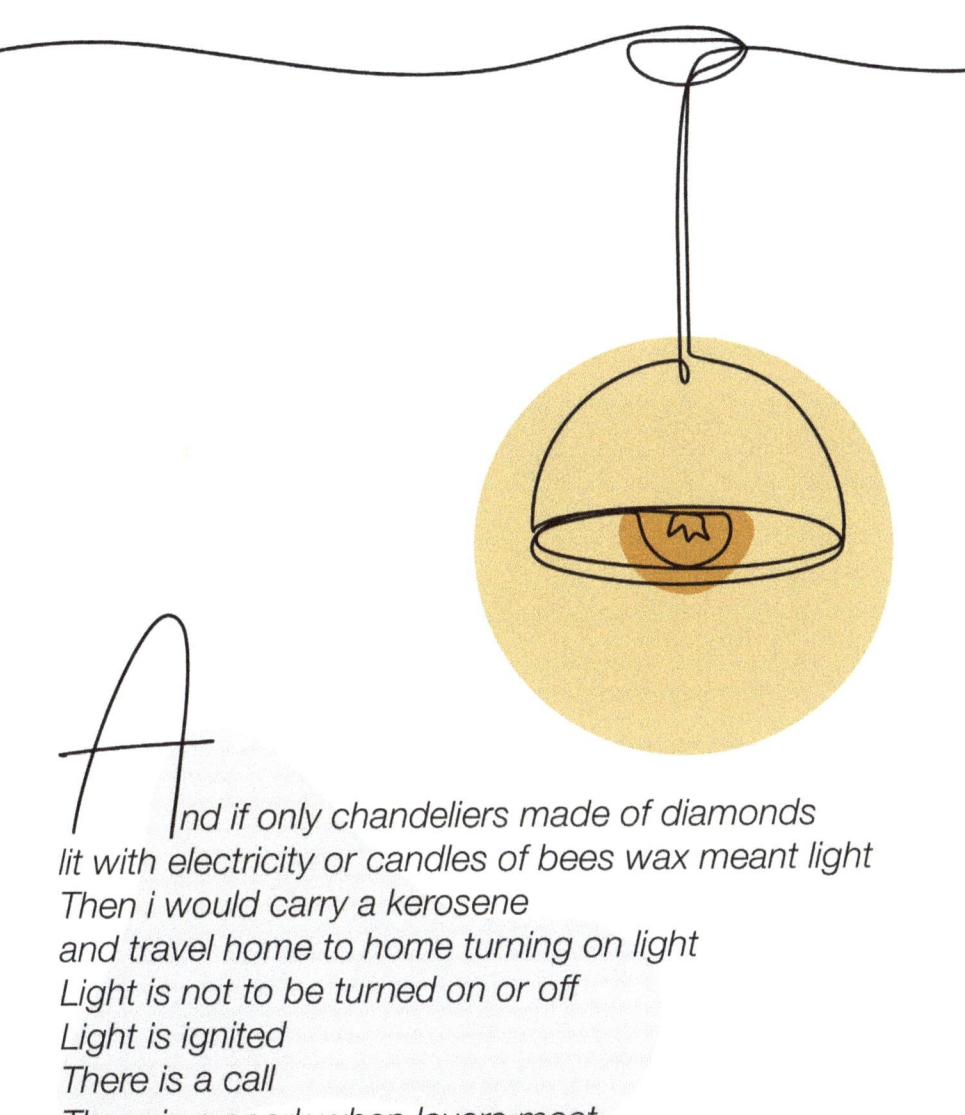

And if only chandeliers made of diamonds
lit with electricity or candles of bees wax meant light
Then i would carry a kerosene
and travel home to home turning on light
Light is not to be turned on or off
Light is ignited
There is a call
There is a spark when lovers meet

If lovers were to be depicted
as man and wife
or man and man
or woman and she
The world would be full of lovers
But somehow there is an essence
in Thee and I and
I and Thee
This essence is the most romantic relation of all
All accepting
All encompassing
All Love

www.ingramcontent.com/pod-product-compliance
Lightning Source LLC
Chambersburg PA
CBHW041544120626
46551CB00019B/2831